THE
ANCIENT
MAYA

*S*pecial thanks to Elin Danien and Isabelle Gordon

CULTURES OF THE PAST

THE ANCIENT MAYA

IRENE FLUM GALVIN

BENCHMARK BOOKS

MARSHALL CAVENDISH

NEW YORK

For my husband, Tom,
and my children, Rachel and Danny

Benchmark Books
Marshall Cavendish Corporation
99 White Plains Road
Tarrytown, New York 10591-9001

© Marshall Cavendish Corporation 1997

Library of Congress Cataloging-in-Publication Data

Galvin, Irene Flum.
    The ancient Maya / by Irene Flum Galvin.
        p.   cm. — (Cultures of the past)
    Includes bibliographical references and index.
    ISBN 0-7614-0091-5 (lib. bdg.)
    1. Mayas—History—Juvenile literature. 2. Mayas—Antiquities—Juvenile literature. 3. Central America—Antiquities—Juvenile literature. I. Title. II. Series.
F1435.G165   1997
972.81'016—dc20   95-47478

Printed in Hong Kong

Book design by Carol Matsuyama
Photo research by Ede Rothaus

Front cover: A procession of richly-dressed nobles celebrate the presentation of an heir to the throne. From the murals at Bonampak.
Back cover: A modern Maya woman wears a blouse with traditional embroidery.

Photo Credits

Front cover: courtesy of ©J. J. Foxx; back cover: courtesy of ©Robert Frerck/ Odyssey/Chicago; pages 6–7, 11, 22, 40, 49, 60, 62, 64, 69, 70: ©J. J. Foxx/NYC; pages 9, 20–21, 29, 55, 58, 63: ©Robert Frerck/Odyssey/Chicago; pages 10, 12, 17, 25, 61, 65: ©DDB Stock Photography; pages 13, 24, 46, 48: ©Robert and Linda Mitchell; page 14: ©J. P. Courau/DDB Stock Photography; page 15: ©Wallace Murray/ DDB Stock Photography; pages 26 *(top and bottom),* 28 *(top and bottom),* 38 *(top and bottom),* 42, 44, 52, 53, 54, 68: ©Justin Kerr; page 31: Scala/Art Resource, NY; page 35: ©John Haffner Layden/NYC; pages 36, 37, 50: ©Boltin Picture Library; page 59: John Berry/Gamma Liaison

CONTENTS

CHAPTER ONE

Ruins
in the
Rain Forest

In 1839 writer John Lloyd Stephens and artist Frederick Catherwood rode mules along muddy trails deep into the thick Central American rain forest in search of ancient ruins. Cutting through vines and branches with machetes, they discovered abandoned cities hidden for centuries from human eyes. While monkeys chattered at them from nearby trees, Catherwood stood ankle-deep in mud, wearing gloves to

protect against mosquitoes, sketching the huge carved pyramids and temples. Stephens's four books about his and Catherwood's discoveries became best-sellers, fascinating the world with tales of a mysterious civilization lost in the steaming rain forest.

Since the time that Stephens and Catherwood discovered the civilization of the ancient Maya*, archaeologists have excavated dozens of monuments covered with hieroglyphs, tombs with treasures, and temples inside of other temples. We now know that the ancient Maya built enormous cities without beasts of burden, metal tools, or the wheel. They created the most complex writing

*The word *Maya* is used both as a noun, as in saying "the Maya," and as an adjective, as in "Maya art." The word *Mayan* is used to refer to language, as in "Mayan language."

Over the centuries, Maya buildings were overgrown by earth, plants, and trees. These mounds cover buildings in Chichén Itzá that have not yet been restored by archaeologists. We can only guess what treasures lie beneath these hills of dirt.

system in the Americas; developed elaborate calendars and a system of mathematics; correctly predicted the movement of the sun, moon, and planets; and produced great works of art.

But why did this astonishingly creative people abandon their cities? Why did their civilization apparently collapse?

There are many things we do not know for certain about how the Maya lived and what they believed. Unlike the ancient Greeks, who have been studied for centuries, the field of Maya studies is relatively new. Discoveries are being made all the time, and scholars interpret the findings in different ways. There are some things we will probably never know. But perhaps that adds to the magic of the Maya.

In the past thirty years, an explosion of interest in the ancient Maya has led to major new finds of ruins and art. One of the most exciting developments is the deciphering of ancient Maya hieroglyphs (pictures or symbols used to represent words or sounds). We can now read much of what the Maya wrote on their monuments and in their books. Though we are not sure of the meanings of all the glyphs, reading the words of this ancient people adds another dimension to our understanding of them. We glimpse clues here and there, and try to interpret them as best we can through our modern eyes. One thing is certain: The more we learn about the Maya, the more intriguing they are—and the more we want to know.

Early Roots: The Preclassic Period

The ancestors of the Maya were Asian peoples who crossed the Bering land bridge from Siberia to Alaska over twelve thousand years ago. They settled in Mesoamerica, an area extending from Mexico to Costa Rica. At first they lived by hunting and gathering food. By 2000 B.C.E.* they had learned to plant crops and had settled in villages on the Pacific coast of Chiapas, Mexico, and Guatemala, near the present Guatemala City.

---

*Many systems of dating have been used by different cultures throughout history. This series of books uses B.C.E. (Before Common Era) and C.E. (Common Era) instead of B.C. (Before Christ) and A.D. (Anno Domini) out of respect for the diversity of the world's peoples.

HOW WE KNOW ABOUT THE MAYA

Many people contribute to our understanding of the Maya. Archaeologists dig up and study the remains of buildings and artifacts. Experts in other fields also study the evidence. Epigraphers are people who love figuring out codes. In the last thirty years, they have made remarkable progress in decoding ancient Maya hieroglyphs. Today about half of the glyphs can be sounded out and understood. Ethnohistorians record the beliefs and customs of the descendants of the ancient Maya. Anthropologists, geographers, art historians, and linguists all contribute their perspectives to understanding how the Maya civilization grew and why it collapsed.

Some 3,500 archaeological sites have been found, yet only a few have been investigated fully. We have much left to learn about the Maya—which makes the search for clues and interpretations even more exciting.

Maya hieroglyphs found in Palenque, Mexico. These hieroglyphs, which were carved between 600 and 900 C.E., show the Maya calendar.

From 2000 B.C.E. to 250 C.E., a period scholars call the Preclassic, the Maya established villages throughout the highlands of southern Mexico, Guatemala, Honduras, and El Salvador, and in the central lowlands of Guatemala, a region called the Petén. During this time their art and religious ideas were influenced by other Mesoamerican peoples, such as the Olmec, great traders who lived along the Gulf Coast of Mexico.

In the late Preclassic period, from 400 B.C.E. to 250 C.E., Maya life changed radically. In both the lowlands and the highlands, villages expanded into city centers with large populations. Some of the biggest buildings in pre-Columbian America were built during this time, such as the huge city center at El Mirador in Guatemala. In Cerros, on the Bay of Chetumal in present-day Belize, the Maya built temples with terraced stairways and carved representations of the sun and Venus. Other sites included Nakbe and Tikal, which played a major role during the following six hundred years.

In the southern coastal area and in the highlands, the Maya built the cities of Izapa, Abaj Takalik, and Kaminaljuyú (kah-mee-nahl-hoo-YOO). The buildings here were smaller than in the lowlands, but they were accompanied by the first monuments with hieroglyphic writing, calendar dates, and images of rulers performing rituals. We do not know the names of individual kings or their histories, but we do know from the scenes carved on sculptures that a small, powerful group dominated society, passing authority down to their children. This pattern of life continued for the next thousand years.

Stone carving from Kaminaljuyú, near Guatemala City. This area was the largest and most powerful Maya site in the highlands during the Late Preclassic period. Kaminaljuyú *means "Place of the Ancient Ones."*

The Age of Kings: The Classic Period

Maya civilization reached its greatest heights from 250 to 900 C.E., an era archaeologists call the Classic period. During this time powerful kings built dozens of great city-states throughout the Maya lowlands, from Tikal in the central area, to Palenque in the west, Copán in the southeast, and Calakmul in the north.

The population exploded to more than two million, intensive farming methods were developed to support the population, and trade routes expanded. This was the period when the Maya built huge temples and pyramids; developed elaborate religious beliefs; and invented accurate, complex systems of writing, mathematics, and astronomy.

Each city-state had its own king and a small group of nobles who ruled over the rest of the people, most of whom were farmers. The rival city-states shared a common cultural background and were often linked through marriages and alliances, but they never united under one ruler. As the population grew, the city-states frequently went to war with one another because of conflicts over trade routes and farmland. The balance of power shifted many times. A single city-state controlled an area for a time, then another became dominant. But no one state ever ruled the entire region.

Palenque, one of the great Maya city-states and one of the best-preserved. It was first discovered in 1746 by a Spanish priest looking for new farmland. To the left is the Palace with its tower. To the right is the Temple of the Inscriptions, which holds the tomb of Pacal, one of Palenque's mightiest rulers.

The Reign of Tikal

One of the most powerful city-states was Tikal, in Guatemala, which was founded during the Preclassic period. Possibly the largest of the Classic-period sites, Tikal covered about 6 square miles (15.5 square kilometers) and had some three thousand constructions. These included temples, pyramids, palaces, shrines, ball courts, plazas, reservoirs, and houses, all linked by broad roads called *sacbe* (SAHK-bay). At the time of its greatest glory, from the fifth century to its decline in the tenth century, some 55,000 people may have lived there. (Estimates of population are based on the number of house mounds—the remains of houses that once stood.)

Some of the restored ruins of Tikal in the jungles of Guatemala. The North Acropolis is a huge platform that covers 2.5 acres (1 hectare). Eight temples were built on it over a period of 300 years (ca. 250–550 C.E.). Older buildings lie buried beneath the buildings visible in the picture.

From carvings and hieroglyphs, we now know some of the history of Tikal. In 411 a man named Stormy Sky became king of the great city. (Most of the names of rulers are nicknames, based on the hieroglyphs, given by modern researchers.) During Stormy

Sky's rule, Tikal controlled a huge area. Located at the center of the east-west trade route across the Maya lowlands, Tikal was apparently a major religious center. People from Yaxchilán (yash-chee-LAHN), Copán, and Quiriguá may have made pilgrimages to Tikal during this time. Tikal's power did not last, however; in 562 the city-state of Caracol defeated Tikal.

For a hundred years Tikal was silent—no new buildings were constructed and no new writings were carved in stone. In 682, a new ruler, Ah Cacau (ah cah-CAW) (also known as Ruler A), ascended to the throne and, in 695, captured the king of Calakmul, Jaguar Paw. Since Calakmul was then probably Tikal's greatest enemy, this marked the restoration of Tikal to its former glory. Ah Cacau celebrated his victory by building many new temples, some of which he dedicated to Stormy Sky, showing his link to his powerful ancestor. Ah Cacau died around 723 and was buried in Temple I, a pyramid over ten stories high with a temple on top. On the roof of the temple, at the top of a great stairway, a sculpture shows Ah Cacau sitting on his throne, looking out over the Great Plaza of Tikal.

After 889 the great city-state lost its power. Abandoned by its people, its immense monuments and temples were gradually overgrown by the rain forest and were hidden for almost a thousand years.

Copán

By the end of the Classic period, hundreds of cities, large and small, were ruled by kings who competed with one another. In Copán, the most southern Maya city, Smoke Jaguar

Tikal Temple I. The tomb of Ah Cacau is underneath the building. A long, narrow stairway leads up to a three-room temple. On top of the temple a huge roofcomb shows the ruler seated on his throne.

ruled from 628 to 695. He was followed by a king named 18 Rabbit, who, in 738, was captured and sacrificed by Cauac Sky of Quiriguá. This must have shocked the Maya world, since Quiriguá was a small city that had probably been under Copán's control.

The Hieroglyphic Stairway at Copán names all the rulers of Copán and tells of their accomplishments. The sculptured figures that stand out from the hieroglyphs carved on the steps are the most important kings dressed in warrior costumes.

Copán regained some of its prestige by making an alliance with the powerful western kingdom of Palenque when a woman from Palenque married the new king of Copán. The people of Copán then built the immense Temple of the Hieroglyphic Stairway as a way of asserting their power. Yax Pac (yash pock), who came to the throne in 763, was the last of the great rulers of Copán.

Palenque

Though most leaders were men, some women held great power as royal wives, princesses, or regents. In Palenque, a city-state in the northwest Maya area, two women were the supreme rulers. Lady Kanal Ikal, the great-grandmother of king Pacal, ruled Palenque, as did Lady Zac Kuk, the mother of Pacal.

Pacal assumed the throne at the age of twelve and ruled from 615 to 683. He and his son, Chan Bahlum, constructed the marvelous Temple of the Inscriptions and the three-temple Group of the Cross at Palenque. After Chan Bahlum's death in 702, three other rulers led Palenque until it, too, lost its power and faded into the mists of the rain forest.

End of a Glorious Era: The Postclassic Period

In about the year 900 the city-states of the Classic period were abandoned. This is often referred to as the "collapse" of the Maya. But the Maya people did not disappear: They moved north to the Yucatán Peninsula, where their civilization flourished until the arrival of the Spaniards in 1521.

Between 800 and 1000 power centered on Uxmal and its neighbors in the hilly Puuc region. Uxmal's only identified ruler was Lord Chac, who reigned in the late ninth and early tenth centuries. He is believed to have built the Governor's Palace, which was probably a ruling council house, and the so-called Nunnery Quadrangle, a group of four residential buildings.

Sculpture of Pacal, greatest king of Palenque. The portrait shows the long nose and flat forehead the Maya considered beautiful. He wears an elaborate headdress and his ears are pierced for ear ornaments.

WHY THE MAYA CIVILIZATION COLLAPSED

No one knows for sure why the Maya abandoned the huge city-states that once formed the core of their world. Overpopulation, combined with not enough good farmland, may have led the Maya to leave lands that no longer provided enough food for their people. Some archaeologists have found evidence of a drought at about the time the lowland city-states were abandoned.

Or perhaps war was the cause. Before the mid–eighth century, battles were limited to seizing power and taking royal captives for sacrifice. After that, warfare became more general, leading to widespread destruction of lives and property. Rivalries among competing city-states may have erupted into civil war.

In earlier times, however, the Maya had also left their cities and moved to new areas. Perhaps they were simply repeating the pattern.

We may never know the real reason—or reasons—for the collapse. But that doesn't stop people from trying to figure it out. Archaeologists dig for clues, epigraphers translate hieroglyphs, and amateurs, too, study the Maya and come up with their own ideas—all trying to solve the mystery.

The Puuc region suffered the same fate as the southern lowlands: Around 1000 the cities were abandoned. Power moved northeast to the flat plains of the Yucatán. This was another time of great change. A Maya group called the Putún (or Chontal) Maya arrived from the Tabasco coast of Mexico. They were warriors, merchants, and sailors who wanted to seize control of resources and trade routes. One Putún group called the Itzá established a capital at Chichén Itzá, which is still known by its original name. As a result of the influence of the Itzá, the Maya incorporated Mexican cultural traditions into their art and architecture in Chichén Itzá.

Chichén Itzá dominated the northern lowlands for more than two hundred years—with a very different form of government from that commonly found during the Classic period. The northern lowlands were ruled not by a single king, but by three or four brothers who shared power in a supreme council. (We do not

SOCIETY IN POSTCLASSIC YUCATÁN

During the Preclassic and Classic periods, Maya society was divided into two classes: nobles (including kings), and commoners. According to Diego de Landa, the Spanish bishop who wrote a book about the Maya, Maya society in the Yucatán during the Postclassic period (900–1500) was made up of four classes: nobles, priests, commoners, and slaves.

The nobles ruled over the other classes, usually passing power down from father to son. The most common form of government was rule by a single nobleman, called a *halach uinic,* or "true man." In other cities a council of nobles ruled.

Like the king of the Classic period, the *halach uinic* was called *ahau* or *k'ul ahau,* which means "king" or "great lord." He was the chief political and religious leader. He appointed the town and village chiefs, probably choosing his younger brothers and cousins for the most important posts. Power was hereditary, just as in Classic times: When the *halach uinic* died, his eldest son succeeded him.

Below the *halach uinic* were the *batabob,* or lesser lords, who ruled the towns and villages. They commanded their own soldiers, presided over a local council of nobles, and served as judges. They were also in charge of seeing that their towns paid tribute to the *halach uinic.* Under them were town councillors who ruled smaller areas of the town, and assistants who carried out the orders of the rulers.

Priests, too, came from the noble class. The second sons of the lords often became know for sure if they were actually brothers, or if they just called themselves that.) It is believed that this form of government contributed to the success of Chichén Itzá.

In the thirteenth century some of the Itzá founded a new city at Mayapán, west of Chichén Itzá. Around 1221 the ruler of Mayapán, Hunac Ceel (hoo-NOK keel), conquered Chichén Itzá, and Mayapán became the power in the Yucatán. Unlike most other Maya cities, Mayapán was walled, leading modern scholars to conclude that warfare was constant. For nearly 250 years, Mayapán ruled the north until the mid–fifteenth century, when it, too, fell.

During the late Postclassic period, other Maya groups such as the Quiché (kee-CHAY) and Cakchiquel (cock-chee-KELL) lived in the highland areas of Guatemala, often fighting one another for control

Maya social classes. At the top was the king, then the nobles and priests. Under them were the lesser lords, who ruled over villages, and craftspeople. Most Maya were corn farmers, who also built the great temples. At the bottom of the social ladder were the slaves.

priests, as did the sons of priests. The high priest advised the lords, performed ceremonies in temples, and wrote the sacred books. He also taught other priests how to keep the ancient calendars, cure diseases, write with hieroglyphs, read the stars, and foretell the future. A town priest was called an *ahkin,* meaning "he of the sun."

Most Maya people were commoners. They worked in the cornfields, supporting themselves and their rulers and priests, and provided the labor to build the ceremonial centers. They also had to give tribute to their rulers, such as vegetables, fish, woven cloth, honey, beeswax, jade beads, and shells.

Slaves were at the bottom of the social ladder. People became slaves by being taken prisoner in war, being born to a slave, or being orphaned. Becoming a slave was also a punishment. If someone was caught stealing, he became a slave for life to the person he had stolen from—unless he was able to pay the person back for what he had stolen.

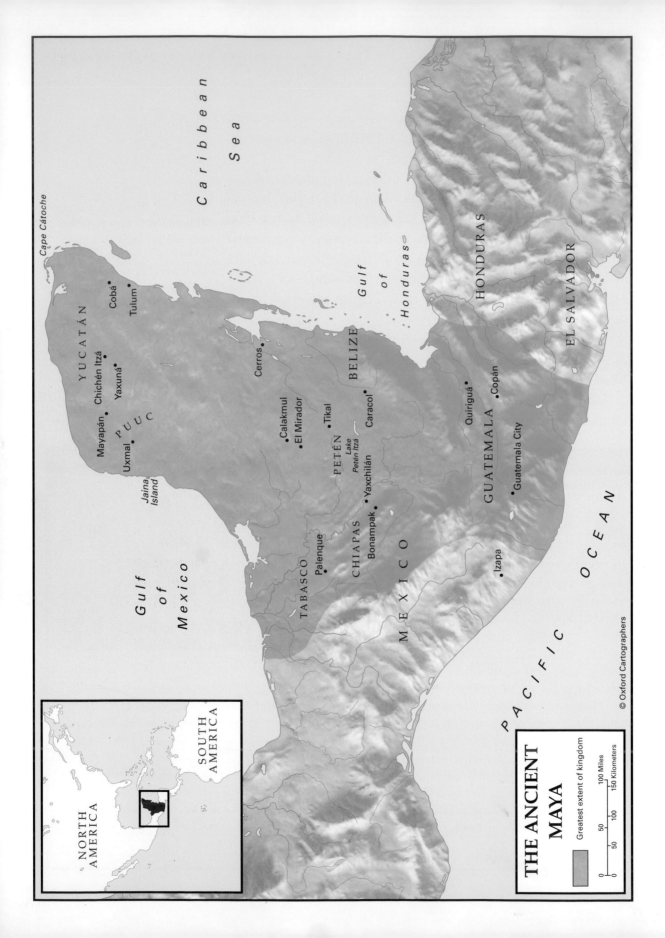

Caribbean Sea

Cape Cátoche

YUCATÁN

Cobá
Tulum

Chichén Itzá
Yaxuná

Mayapán
PUUC
Uxmal

Jaina Island

Gulf of Mexico

Cerros

Calakmul
El Mirador
Tikal
Caracol

PETÉN
Lake Petén Itzá

Yaxchilán

Bonampak

Palenque

CHIAPAS

TABASCO

MEXICO

Izapa

BELIZE

Gulf of Honduras

Honduras

HONDURAS

EL SALVADOR

Quiriguá
Copán

GUATEMALA

Guatemala City

PACIFIC OCEAN

© Oxford Cartographers

NORTH AMERICA

SOUTH AMERICA

THE ANCIENT MAYA

Greatest extent of kingdom

100 Miles
150 Kilometers
50
100
50
0
0

of resources. Their lack of unity helped the Spanish conquer the Maya.

Invasion of the Bearded White Men

In 1502 Christopher Columbus came upon a canoeful of Maya traveling in the Gulf of Honduras—the first contact between Europeans and the Maya. In 1517 Francisco Hernandez de Cordoba led an expedition of Spaniards to the northernmost tip of the Yucatán, known as Cape Catoche (kah-TOH-chay). The Spaniards were looking for gold, glory, and to spread Christianity.

By 1524 the Spaniards were at war with the Maya. Though the Maya resisted the conquest of their land, they were overwhelmed by Spanish guns, horses, and diseases. The Spaniards also used rival Maya groups to fight against one another. In 1546 the Yucatán was conquered. However, one group of Maya, the Itzá who lived near Lake Petén Itzá, held out against the invaders for another 150 years until 1697.

The Spaniards forced the Maya to accept Christianity and Spanish rule. One Spanish bishop, Diego de Landa, burned hundreds of Maya books. Thousands of Maya men, women, and children died as a result of warfare, famine, and disease. Forced to work as slaves for the Spanish, they lost their land and their freedom.

About five million Maya today live on the same lands where their ancestors lived. Most of them struggle against poverty, malnutrition, discrimination, and governments that do not represent them, nor respect their rights. In spite of modern problems, the glories of this ancient civilization are still visible in the art and architecture left behind, and in the beliefs and customs of the Maya's descendants.

CHAPTER TWO

MYSTERIOUS MESSAGES IN STONE

Understanding Maya culture is like putting together an elaborate jigsaw puzzle, but without any idea of how the picture should look when it's finished. Researchers dust off the dirt of a thousand years from temples, carvings, and ancient writing, and interpret them as best they can. Though our picture of the Maya is incomplete, the pieces we have been able to fill in offer a fascinating glimpse of this ancient civilization.

Postclassic city of Tulúm on the east coast of the Yucatán Peninsula in Mexico. El Castillo, the major temple, overlooks the Caribbean Sea. Maya sailors used to land their canoes on the beach below the walled city. First occupied around 1200 C.E., it was probably a trading center.

Architecture

The first thing that catches the eye as we look at ancient Maya culture is their majestic architecture. For about fifteen hundred years, starting about 600 B.C.E., the Maya constructed huge stone buildings around open plazas paved with sparkling white plaster. Temples towered on top of giant pyramids as high as ten-story buildings, with stairways up the front. Maya rulers and priests probably walked up the narrow stairways wearing colorful costumes and carrying gifts for the gods. Though the temples are white today, in the time of the ancient Maya they were painted with brilliant colors. We can imagine the king inside the brightly painted temple performing religious ceremonies, while the people gathered in the broad courtyard below.

Beneath the pyramids lay the sealed tombs of kings. One of

the most remarkable tombs that has been uncovered is that of Pacal, the king of Palenque. Discovered in 1949, the tomb deep beneath the Temple of the Inscriptions enclosed a large sarcophagus, or stone coffin. Within the sarcophagus was the skeleton of a man adorned with royal jade jewelry, including a mask of jade. Pictures and writing on the side of the sarcophagus showed Pacal's ancestors and the dates of their deaths. The sculptured scene on the cover showed the king falling backward into the underworld.

Palaces, made up of groups of buildings around small plazas, are found at almost every Maya site. Built on low platforms, the palaces enclose interconnected rooms and doorways.

The lid of Pacal's sarcophagus shows the dead king on the setting sun as he falls into the jaws of the earth monster, representing the underworld. He falls along the World Tree, which is visible behind his body. Hieroglyphs on the sarcophagus tell Pacal's birth date, date of death, and the names of his ancestors. The tomb was discovered buried deep inside the Temple of the Inscriptions at Palenque. It took three years to clear out the rubble in the staircase and find the tomb.

They were probably used as administrative offices, to receive visitors, and as homes for the ruling nobles. In some palaces, such as the one at Palenque, a throne looks through doorways onto courtyards. The royal family probably sat on the large throne to greet the people and answer their requests for favors.

The largest city-states, such as Tikal, had many other plazas besides the central plaza, with hundreds of stone buildings in all. These groups of buildings were linked by paved roads so broad that, as the Spaniards wrote, ten horsemen could ride side by side on them. The roads, often half a mile long (0.8 kilometers), were probably used for religious processions. The longest road connected two major city-states, Cobá and Yaxuná, in the northern Yucatán. It was over sixty miles (ninety-six kilometers) long and perfectly straight.

How did the Maya build such monumental pyramid-temples and palaces without oxen or horses to pull heavy weights, and without carts with wheels to carry building materials long distances? We can only imagine how hard people must have worked cutting stone, carrying it, and piling it into the pyramids we admire today.

Art

Like the great temples, Maya art was commissioned by the king. Art had an important purpose: to communicate messages to the king's subjects. The king was portrayed as the center of the universe; without the rituals he performed, the universe would fall into chaos. Certain images were repeated over and over: the king taking the throne, going to war, and sacrificing captives. Public art was like a billboard to show that kings were essential to maintain balance between the human world and the supernatural world of the gods. It was also created to ensure that the king would be remembered forever.

Unfortunately only art made of lasting materials such as stone, stucco (a kind of plaster), clay, and shell have survived the years. Some scraps of textiles and a few musical instruments have been found, but what must have been a majestic tradition of weaving, feather work, and the making of musical instruments has left hardly a trace.

Oval Palace Tablet. Pacal, on the right, sits on a double-headed jaguar throne. His mother, Lady Zac Kuk, sits on the floor to his left. She hands him a headdress as part of the ceremony crowning him king of Palenque.

Sculpture

The Maya covered the walls and doors of their buildings with sculptures of gods, kings, and captives. Huge masks of gods often covered whole walls, such as at the temple at Cerros in Belize. Built about 50 B.C.E., the temple walls on both sides of the stairway were covered by four giant stucco masks. The bottom two were jaguar faces representing the sun god, while the top two were masks of the god of the planet Venus.

The Maya also carved freestanding monuments called stelae (STEE-lee), or stone pillars, which they placed in rows in front of temples. The carvings on the stelae usually show a single standing figure, with hieroglyphs giving historical information and dates. Carved to record important events in the lives of the rulers of the Maya city-states, the images show battles, celebrations, sacrifices, and kings taking the throne. The tradition of erecting dated stelae lasted for about six hundred years.

The first dated stela, called Stela 29, is from Tikal. On one side it shows a richly dressed Maya ruler wearing jade ornaments. The other side bears a date equivalent to our year 292 C.E. This stela is considered especially important by archaeologists because it defines the Classic period, the time when carved monuments were first dated.

The Maya also carved thrones, benches, and large stone objects that may be altars. One altar at Copán shows sixteen rulers sitting one next to the other, with the oldest ancestor facing the newest. This is believed to show that the newest ruler received the right to rule from the honored, sometimes legendary, ancestors who founded the city.

Altar Q at Copán shows the sixteen rulers of Copán each sitting cross-legged on a hieroglyph of his name. Yax Kuk Mo', the founder of Copán, hands the scepter of office to Yax Pac, the sixteenth ruler, proving Yax Pac's right to rule.

Painted ceramic pot shows supernatural jaguar serpent and bearded dragon.

Pottery, Figurines, and Jade

The Maya were highly skilled at making pottery and decorating it with detailed drawings and hieroglyphs. Often found in tombs and painted many colors, these ceramics show the sacrifice of captives, dances, and celebrations of new kings taking power. They also show gods and pictures of the underworld. Some of the scenes illustrate stories told by the Maya in their sacred book, the *Popol Vuh* (see page 40).

Thanks to advances in deciphering Maya hieroglyphs, we can read more and more of the words on these vessels. A hieroglyph on one was recently deciphered as "chocolate"—a precious drink enjoyed only by the kings and nobles. This interpretation of the glyph was confirmed when scientists found remains of chocolate in the bottom of the vessel.

The Maya also made small clay figurines of lords and ladies, warriors, rulers on thrones, dancers, ballplayers, and gods. The most finely made ones were found in tombs on Jaina (HIGH-nah) Island, placed in the hands of the dead. Rarely more than eleven inches (twenty-eight centimeters) tall, they were brightly painted and either shaped by hand or in a mold. Those made in a mold sometimes contained small pellets to make a rattle, or a mouthpiece and holes so that they could be played as an ocarina (a simple wind instrument). The details are so fine on these figurines that you can see the tattoo on a face no bigger than a fingernail!

Jade, a precious stone, was valued as highly as money is today. Nobles wore jade jewelry as ear ornaments, bracelets, necklaces, and anklets, and were often buried with jade ornaments. It is remarkable that the Maya were able to carve jade—it is a very hard stone, and the Maya did not use metal tools. The fine carvings were made by rubbing cords across the jade, using water and small particles of stone to cut into the gem. Imagine the patience it took to make just one small figure!

One special type of jade carving was the celt (sehlt), which was oval-shaped like an ear of corn. It is believed by some scholars that the celt was originally an image of corn, which was

Figurine from Jaina Island of male from the upper class of society. He wears a turbanlike headdress also worn by scribes.

THE BALL GAME

The next time you play a game with a rubber ball think of the Maya. Like other Mesoamerican peoples, they played a game with a rubber ball, which was the granddaddy of all modern rubber-ball games. But though we call it a ball game, their game was completely unlike ours today.

Almost every Maya city had a ball court. Located near the king's palace, it ranged from the size of a volleyball court to a football field. The playing area, shaped like an I, was a narrow alley between sloping walls with two end zones. The ball was made of solid rubber and was very heavy. It was larger than a basketball and probably bounced higher than any ball you've ever seen.

Although we do not know all the rules of the game, we believe players competed to hit the ball off the sloping walls of the ball court. Some ball courts had stone rings along the sides, which may have been the targets. Players could not use their hands; they could only use their hips, thighs, shoulders, or upper arms. Since the ball was so heavy, they wore knee and elbow pads and special padding around their waists to protect themselves. In artwork we see images of players throwing themselves to the ground and lunging to hit the ball with their hips—perhaps because they would lose if the ball hit the floor of the playing area.

The Maya ball game was not a sport as we understand it. It was actually a religious ritual in which losers lost more than the game—they lost their lives. The game was probably played between the nobles of a city and the high-born warriors or king of a neighboring city who had been captured in raids. The captives would be forced to play—and, of course, to lose—showing the power of one city over the other. When they lost, they were sacrificed as an offering to the gods.

When they played this game, Maya kings and warriors were acting out a scene from Maya myth. In the story the Hero Twins played ball with the gods of death in the underworld—and defeated them. (See page 41). By playing the ball game, Maya nobles identified themselves with the ancient heroes who won over evil. It's also possible that the game symbolized the movement of the sun and moon (which the Hero Twins became). The ball was kept in constant motion in the air, just as the sun and moon move and turn in the sky.

Early Spanish historians wrote about the ball game as it was played at Chichén Itzá, which had the largest ball court in Mesoamerica. According to their reports, it was so difficult for players to get the ball through the ring on the side of the court that when one of them did, the spectators had to give the lucky player all their clothing and jewelry. As a result, as soon as the ball was hit through the ring, all the spectators would try to run away—while the friends of the player ran after them to collect the prize!

valued very highly since it was an important food. Corn was perishable, but a celt made of green jade would last.

Painting

Extraordinary paintings found in Bonampak, Mexico, give us a unique look at royal life among the Maya around the year 790. Most paintings from so long ago have disintegrated, but these paintings survived because a mineral called calcite accidentally dripped on them and preserved them.

The brightly colored murals cover the walls of three rooms. In one room pictures show a battle in the jungle, with the winning king wearing a jaguar skin and taking a noble prisoner. Other rooms show the presentation of the heir to the throne, prisoners being tortured, and the king and nobles wearing feather head-dresses and dancing in victory. Nearby, musicians blow horns, strike turtle shells and drums, and shake rattles.

These paintings were recently cleaned, and computer reconstructions of them were made. As a result it's now possible to see more clearly than ever these unique pictures of rituals performed to celebrate an heir's right to the throne.

Jade was highly prized by the Maya. These ear ornaments and ring probably belonged to a ruler or noble.

Writing

One of the most significant achievements of the Maya was their creation of the first complete writing system in the Americas. They wrote everywhere—on buildings, bones, shells, pottery, paintings, stone monuments, and in books. Their writing baffled scholars for years, since they used complex hieroglyphs, which are pictures or symbols used to represent words or sounds. At first scholars could decipher only Maya numbers, so they believed the Maya wrote only about time and dates. Today, however, about 80 percent of the glyphs have been deciphered.

This jade celt, the Leyden Plaque, shows a portrait of a king of Tikal, Moon Zero Bird, standing over a captive. Writing on the celt says that the king was "seated," or came to the throne, in 320. He wears a royal belt with dangling jade celts—one of which may be the Leyden Plaque itself.

Brightly painted murals in Bonampak show the Maya rituals celebrating the designation of the heir to the throne. In a great procession, members of the court wear elaborate costumes and musicians play a drum, rattles, and turtle shells.

We now know that the glyphs tell the story of the great deeds of Maya rulers and the rivalries between Maya city-states. By comparing this written history with archaeological evidence, researchers find new clues to unlock the mysteries of the Maya.

Unscrambling a Puzzle

The longest known inscription in Mayan writing is found on a huge stairway at Copán. Each step of the staircase is carved with glyphs—2,200 of them. Over time, many of the steps fell or crumbled, so archaeologists are working to unscramble and restore them. The stairway names all the rulers of Copán and their victories. By tracing the royal line back to the founder of Copán, the stairway was intended to assert that Copán was still power-ful—even though a king had recently been captured and sacri-ficed by a rival city-state.

Maya Books

Imagine how much we would know about the Maya if we could read their books—their history, their myths, their stories about daily life. They did write books—hundreds and perhaps thou-sands of them—and treasured them as sacred objects. But only four have survived.

One reason so few have lasted is that they were made of paper from fig-tree bark, which crumbles in humid weather. But another reason is the fanaticism of a Spanish bishop.

After the Spanish conquest, friars set out to convert the Maya to Christianity. The bishop of Yucatán, Diego de Landa, befriended a Maya chief, who trusted him enough to show him the secret, sacred books of his people. Some years later Landa burned as many of the Maya books as he could find, saying that there was nothing in them that was not the work of the devil. But a strange thing happened: This man, who single-handedly destroyed what would have been a treasure-house of information about the Maya, later wrote a book about them. This book is today one of the most important sources of information about the Maya.

Three of the books that survived were sent to Europe by Spanish colonists. They are called the Madrid, Paris, and Dresden

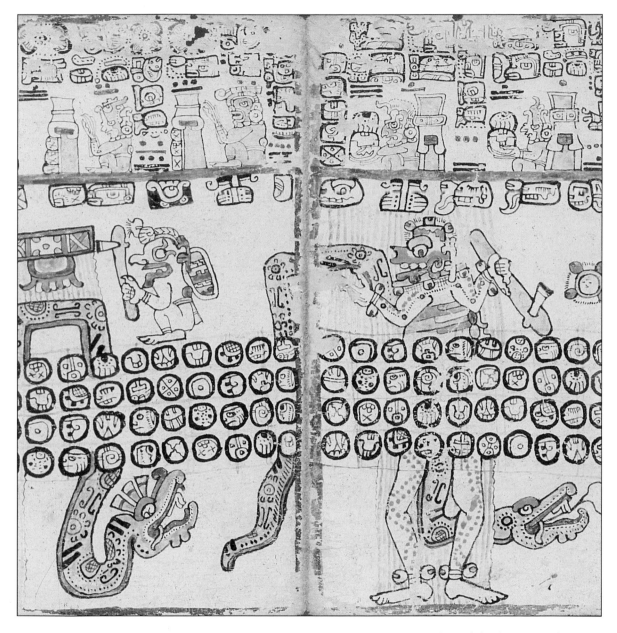

Codices, after the cities where they are presently located. A fourth, found in a cave in Mexico, is a fragment called the Grolier Codex. All four have astronomical information that was used to predict eclipses and determine days of good and bad luck. The Dresden Codex, which was written in the twelfth century, predicts solar eclipses accurate to within one day over four hundred years.

One of the four Maya books that have survived time, weather, and the wrath of a Spanish bishop. The Madrid Codex contains horoscopes and almanacs used by priests to predict the future and the best times to hold sacred ceremonies.

Numbers and Days

Maya numbers look different from ours because the Maya wrote them with a system of bars and dots. A dot represents the number one, a bar stands for five, and a shell stands for zero. With these symbols the Maya could write any number. For example, a bar and three dots is eight. Two bars and two dots equals twelve.

The Maya were the first known people in the world to develop the concept of zero. It was an important part of their number system since it allowed them to use place value to write their numbers. For example, how would you write the number 420 if you didn't have a zero to hold the place of the ones?

When we write numbers, we count by tens. The Maya counted by twenties, probably from counting both fingers and toes. Their place value went from bottom to top, not from right to left as ours does. Take the number 25. In our system, the 2 stands for 2 tens (or 20), and the 5 stands for 5 ones (or 5). To write the number 25 in Maya math, you would write a bar for the 5, and, leaving a space above it, you would write one dot, representing 20. (See if you can read the Maya numbers on page 33.)

Calendars

For the Maya, calendars were not just tools to keep track of time. Days and numbers were associated with deities, who influenced people's lives. Those who understood the calendars held a key to understanding the powers that controlled each day, which meant they could predict events. The ruling nobles probably used their knowledge of the calendars to maintain power and prestige in the eyes of the common people.

Three separate calendars were used for different purposes: the sacred round, a solar calendar, and the Long Count.

The sacred round was a year of 260 days, consisting of 20 day names and 13 numbers. Each day had a day name and a number, such as 1 Akbal, 2 Kan, and 3 Chicchan. This is similar to our calendar with 7 day names and 30 or 31 numbers. Each of the 260 days was associated with a deity who was believed to influence people born on that day. The sacred round was used to plan religious ceremonies.

The solar calendar had 365 days divided into 18 months of

CAN YOU READ MAYA NUMBERS?

Here are the Maya numbers from 1 to 15. (A dot is 1, a bar is 5, and a shell is 0).

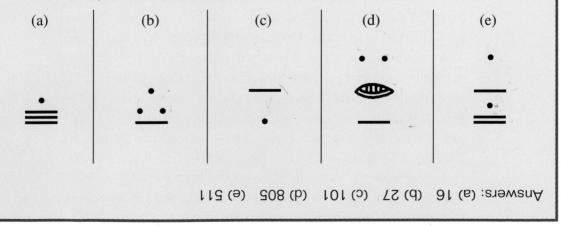

Remember that Maya place value goes up by twenties, not by tens as in our number system. Also, remember that you read the numbers from the bottom up. For example, here is the number 445:

(400s)	•	= 400
(20s)	• •	= 40
(1s)	—	= 5

Now see if you can tell what these numbers are:

(a)   (b)   (c)   (d)   (e)

Answers: (a) 16 (b) 27 (c) 101 (d) 805 (e) 511

33

20 days each, with a short month of 5 days (which were considered unlucky days) at the end of the year. Some of the month names were Pop, Uo, Zip, Zotz, and Tzec.

Each day had two names: its sacred-round name and its name in the solar calendar. A particular day, such as 8 Ahau 12 Ceh, would occur only once in fifty-two years. (8 Ahau is a day name in the sacred round; 12 Ceh is a day name in the solar calendar.) The ending of a cycle and beginning of a new one was celebrated as a major festival. Dates on monuments are always given according to both calendars.

The third Maya calendar is called the Long Count. This counted days from a fixed starting point—August 13, 3114 B.C.E., the day the Maya believed the universe began. The Maya counted thousands of years into the past from this date to show a king's connection with ancestors and gods, and thus his right to rule. They also counted ahead to the future: Pacal, the king of Palenque, had the eightieth anniversary of his coming to power (July 29, 615 C.E.) carved on a tablet in the Temple of the Inscriptions. He could count so far ahead that, according to our system, Pacal recorded the date October 23, 4772.

Astronomy

Without telescopes the Maya watched the skies and kept precise records of what they saw. They considered the planets and stars to be deities. They believed that by tracking the heavenly bodies, they would see patterns that would predict the future. The movements of the stars told the kings when to go to war, celebrate a royal marriage, take the throne, and hold religious rituals. The Maya were so accurate in their observations that they could predict solar and lunar eclipses, as well as the cycles of Venus.

Some Maya buildings appear to have been built to study the sky, such as the observatory Caracol at Chichén Itzá. Other buildings line up with the path of the sun or stars across the sky. El Castillo, a pyramid at Chichén Itzá, was built so that a shadow cast by the setting sun falls right on the edge of the nine-level staircase on March 21 and September 21, the days of the spring and autumn equinoxes. This creates the image of a snake slither-

ing up the stairway from a stone serpent head at the bottom. The pyramid itself has four staircases with ninety-one steps each, which, added to the top platform, equals 365—the number of days in the solar year.

The Maya also watched the Milky Way, which they called the World Tree. Some researchers believe that Maya myths actually record the movement of the Milky Way. Though this is still open to question, it is certainly true that the Maya's fascination with the sky and stars is closely related to their beliefs about the deities and the purpose of human life.

The Caracol Observatory at Chichén Itzá. A round temple, it contains a spiral staircase that goes up to a small room near the top. The Maya probably observed the sky through windowlike openings in the thick walls. Through the window facing west, it was possible to see the sun set on March 21, the vernal equinox. Other views showed the setting of the moon on the same date.

CHAPTER THREE

GODS AND HEROES

The Maya worshiped many deities. Here the sun god, called Kinich Ahau, is shown in the jaws of the earth god. The elaborately carved piece was used to burn incense as an offering to the gods.

The ancient Maya believed that everything in the universe—people, jaguars, rocks, trees, stars—had a spiritual nature. They saw the world of people and the world of spirits as deeply connected. All parts of life affected one another: The gods influenced people, and people influenced the gods. This connection among things is shown in Maya beliefs, myths, and the way they imagined the universe.

The Four Corners of the Earth

To the Maya the earth was the back of a giant turtle or crocodile floating on the sea. Above it were the starry heavens, and below it was the watery underworld called Xibalbá (shee-bahl-BAH). The gods and spirits that lived in the heavens and Xibalbá were invisible, but human beings could communicate with them through prayer, visions, and sacrifice.

Sometimes the earth was seen as a cornfield or rectangular house with four corners—north, south, east, and west. At each corner stood a different tree, bird, and god. Each direction also was a different color: The east was red, the west black, the north white, and the south yellow.

East was the most important direction because the sun rose there every day. The sun was seen as a god, called Kinich Ahau or Sun-faced Lord. The Maya believed that when the sun set in the west, it descended into the underworld, changed into a jaguar, and passed through many dangers. At dawn it was reborn as the sun to journey across the sky.

A giant blue-green tree, called the World Tree, rose through the center of the universe. The branches of this sacred tree reached up into the heavens, and its roots stretched down into the under-

The Maya believed the earth was a giant turtle or crocodile floating in the sea. In this sculpture, a man—perhaps a god or hero—stands on the turtle's back.

world. The World Tree connected the world of human beings with the invisible world of spirits and gods.

Gods

The Maya believed in many gods with different names, like the god of corn or the god of night. At the same time they believed that all the gods were part of just one spiritual force. It was as though they were one god and many gods at the same time—like different expressions on the same face.

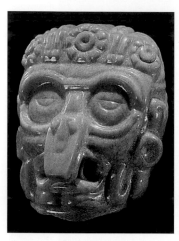

Jade mask of the head of a bird deity. The bird god was one of the earliest of Maya deities. In the Popol Vuh, *Vucub Caquix was a bird god who set himself up as a false sun before the beginning of time.*

Maya gods had many names, such as god of the sun, god of night, or god of corn (shown here). Yet the gods were also considered different aspects of the same spiritual force.

In some cases we can identify the names the Maya gave the gods—though the same god sometimes had different names in different cities and during different time periods. Often, though, the names have been given by modern scholars. For example, God B is a name given by scholars, not the Maya name.

Gods were portrayed as men, women, animals, or creatures

SOME MAYA GODS OF POSTCLASSIC TIMES

Itzamna, a Reptile God (God D)

Itzamna was the high god of the Maya, lord of the heavens and lord of day and night. He was thought of as the first priest, the inventor of writing, and the god of medicine. He was sometimes identified as a crocodile, a bird god, a tree, or a very old person with no teeth, sunken cheeks, and a round disk on his forehead. It is believed that the disk was a mirror used for telling the future. Itzamna was probably also known during Postclassic times as Kukulcan, the feathered serpent god known in central Mexico as Quetzalcoatl (kayts-ahl-koh-AH-tuhl).

Chac, the Rain God (God B)

The rain god, Chac, was a friendly god associated with creation and life. Since rain was essential for growing corn, Chac was one of the most important gods to the ordinary Maya farmer. In art he was often shown with a reptile face, a long snout, and curved fangs. He carried the lightning ax, and his power was associated with war and human sacrifice.

Yum Kaax (yoom KAHSH), the Corn God (God E)

The corn god was also a friendly god. The patron of farming, he was always shown as a young man. An ear of corn often sprouted from his head as a head-dress. In myths he was the father of the Hero Twins (see page 41).

Ix Chel, a Rainbow Deity (Goddess I)

Ix Chel was one of the few Maya deities who was female. She was called the rainbow goddess, and was associated with healing, childbirth, and foretelling the future. But she also had a negative side: She was associated with snakes and destruction. The island of Cozumel off the eastern coast of Yucatán was a center of devotion to Ix Chel.

that looked like both a person and an animal. Each day, month, and number was associated with a god. For example, the sun god (God G) watched over the number four, the death god (God A) over the number ten, and the rain god (God B) over the number thirteen.

The *Popol Vuh*

Much of what we know about Maya beliefs comes from the *Popol Vuh* (POH-pole VOO), a sacred book written in the sixteenth century by the Quiché Maya of Guatemala. Like a bible, the *Popol Vuh* (or "Council Book") contains stories that explain life. Two of the stories tell how the world was created and about the legendary ancestors of the Maya, the Hero Twins.

The Story of Creation

Before the world was created, the *Popol Vuh* says, there was just the sky and sea. Then two gods began to talk. They were Gucumatz, or the Sovereign Plumed Serpent, who lived in the water, and Heart of Sky, also called Hurricane, who lived in

Carved image of a feathered serpent deity found at the Temple of the Warriors in Chichén Itzá. One of the two creator gods, Gucumatz is the Maya translation of Quetzalcoatl, a feathered serpent who was one of the great gods of ancient Mesoamerica.

the sky. The words they spoke formed the mountains and earth, trees and plants.

Then they made birds, jaguars, snakes, and all the other animals. The creators asked the animals to praise them, but the animals just squawked and howled. So the creators decided to create people who would worship them.

First they made a person of clay. The person talked, but its words made no sense. Its body was weak and it crumbled. So the gods destroyed the clay person and tried again.

This time they made people of wood. The wooden people looked, spoke, and had children, but they were dry beings without smiles or tears. They lacked souls and understanding, and didn't respect the gods. So Gucumatz and Heart of Sky sent a great flood and destroyed the wooden people. As a reminder of this failed creation, some of the wooden people were allowed to survive—as monkeys.

There were still no people to worship the gods, so Gucumatz and Heart of Sky called on the fox, coyote, parrot, and crow to bring white and yellow corn from the mountains. The gods ground the kernels nine times and made the flesh of the first four men, using water to create human blood. These people of corn were very different from the wooden people: They were wise and understanding and knew how to properly worship the gods.

But Gucumatz and Heart of Sky were still not happy. They worried that the new people were too much like gods, since they could see everywhere and understand everything. So Gucumatz and Heart of Sky clouded the eyes of the men so that they would see only what was nearby. To make up for taking away their perfect vision and understanding, the gods gave the first men beautiful wives. These men and women were the parents of the Quiché Maya people.

The Story of the Hero Twins

The largest part of the *Popol Vuh* is about the Hero Twins, human beings with godlike powers who rid the world of demons and made it safer for the people born after them.

The Hero Twins were Hunahpu (hoo-nah-POOH) and Xbalanque (sh-bah-LAHN-kay). Their father and uncle, also twins,

The Hero Twins appear in Maya sculpture, ceramics, and books. This intricately carved incense burner is probably an image of Hunahpu or Xbalanque. He wears a bird-beak helmet, a beaded necklace, and a cape. He rides on the back of a crocodile creature, and sits on the head of a monkey-faced earth god.

were ballplayers who had been killed by the death gods of the underworld, Xibalbá. Hunahpu and Xbalanque also grew up to be ballplayers, and also went to Xibalbá to play ball with the death gods.

The death gods tried to trick the Hero Twins as they had tricked their father and uncle, but Hunahpu and Xbalanque outwitted them. They passed safely though the House of Gloom, the House of Knives, the House of Cold, the House of Jaguars, and the House of Fire. In the House of Bats, however, Hunahpu peeked out from his blowgun, where he was hiding, and a bat took his head off. Xbalanque made a temporary head for his brother from a squash, and, magically, Hunahpu could see and speak. The twins then went to play ball with the gods. The gods used Hunahpu's real head for a ball, but Xbalanque tricked them and got Hunahpu's real head back.

The twins knew that the death gods would not be satisfied until they died, so they allowed themselves to be sacrificed. The death gods ground their bones and threw them into a river, but the twins were reborn as fish-men and returned to Xibalbá.

Disguised as poor actors, they danced for the gods of Xibalbá. The gods told them to sacrifice a dog and bring it back to life, which they did. The twins then sacrificed a man and brought him back to life. As a final act, Xbalanque cut off Hunahpu's head and brought him back to life. The death gods grew very excited and asked the twins to kill them. The twins gladly killed the death gods—but didn't bring them back to life.

The Hero Twins triumphed over the powers of death—and rose into the heavens where they became the sun and moon (or Venus).

Doorways between Worlds: The Role of Ritual

The Maya believed that people and gods needed each other. People needed the gods to bring rain, make food grow, and create new life. The gods needed people to offer them nourishment and worship them. By following the wishes of the gods, the Maya believed they could keep harmony in the universe and avoid disasters such as earthquakes or hurricanes. The way the Maya communicated with the gods to know their wishes was through ceremonies and ritual.

Blood Offerings

The Maya believed that human beings could nourish the gods with human blood. If the gods were satisfied, life would be good. Important occasions in the life of the individual and the community were celebrated by letting blood (cutting oneself on purpose to make blood flow). For example, after the birth of an heir, the king performed a sacrifice of his own blood.

Letting blood was important because blood nourished the gods, and also because the loss of blood caused visions. For the Maya the highest religious experience was a vision in which a person communicated with the forces of the heavens and Xibalbá.

Kings (and queens) would cut themselves and let their blood drop on pieces of bark, which were then burned. It was believed that the blood-tinged smoke conjured up the gods or ancestors, and that the king would then have a vision. Based on his vision, he would make decisions such as when to go to war.

All people could communicate with the gods through blood offerings, but kings were especially powerful, so their visions were more powerful than other people's. (Also, since Maya art records the deeds of kings, we know more about kings letting blood than about common people letting blood.)

In Maya art, this contact between the human world and supernatural world was shown as a snake called a Vision Serpent,

Bloodletting ceremony. The king of Yaxchilán, Shield Jaguar, holds a torch while his wife Lady Xoc lets blood by pulling a thorn-lined rope through her tongue. The hieroglyphs above and to the left of the king tell the date—9.13.17.15.12 5 Eb 15 Mac, or October 28, 709 C.E.—the king's and queen's names, and the event: "he is letting blood" and "she is letting blood." Lintel 26 from Yaxchilán, Mexico.

ANIMAL COMPANION SPIRITS

The Maya believed that every human being had an animal companion spirit. When a person was born, his or her soul was placed in his or her body, and an identical soul was placed in the body of an animal. The fate of the person and the animal companion were bound together throughout their lives: Whatever happened to one happened to the other. It was believed that people could transform themselves into their animal companion spirits during war or in dreams. Bloodletting also allowed people to conjure up their animal companion spirits.

Pottery scenes from many Maya kingdoms show the animal spirit floating above the king or dancing like a human being. The animal companion of the king was the jaguar. To show his connection with his animal companion, a king wore a jaguar helmet and a jaguar-skin shirt.

The modern Maya also believe that each person has an animal companion spirit. This spirit lives in a corral inside the mountains and is protected by the ancestors. In dreams a person may see or become his or her animal spirit. Shamans, or priests believed to be able to contact the spirit world, have the power to transform themselves into their animal spirits. A powerful shaman may have more than one animal spirit.

If a person behaves badly, the ancestors may let the person's animal spirit out of the corral. If the animal gets injured, the person will, too. Special ceremonies must be performed to get the animal spirit back into the corral.

which reared up over the person letting blood. An example is Lintel 25 on Structure 23 at Yaxchilán, where Lady Xoc (shoke), the wife of the king Shield Jaguar, lets blood and has a vision of a warrior, perhaps an ancestor.

Sacrifice

Sacrifice was another way the Maya contacted the spirit world. This ranged from simple offerings of food to human sacrifice. When a new king took the throne or a building was dedicated, a human sacrifice was considered necessary to seal the event. As far as we know, a city-state did not sacrifice its own people. The Maya went to war for the purpose of taking captives, whom they then sacrificed. This sacrifice often occurred after the playing of the ritual ball game (See page 27.)

Sacrifice was necessary to maintain the process of creation, since the Maya believed that life could only be born from death,

as corn comes from a "dead" seed. In Maya myths even the gods sacrificed themselves, allowing this world to be created. Sacrifice was one way humans played a role in creation.

Holy Places and People

Sacred places, or openings to the world of the spirit, were found everywhere, according to the Maya. Some places were especially sacred, like mountains and caves, because they were openings between the layers of the universe. Temples were built to create sacred spaces where ceremonies could be performed.

The king himself was seen as a living World Tree who was able to make contact between the realms of the universe. During ceremonies the king either took the identity of a god or was thought to actually become a god. A carving at Palenque shows a king wearing a corn headdress and holding an ax, just like the god of corn. The same image is found in the Madrid Codex.

Festivals

Another way the Maya worshiped was by celebrating festivals. They would fast to make themselves pure, burn incense, pray, dance, and make sacrifices. Festivals often revolved around certain days of the year. For example, the end of each twenty-year period (according to the sacred-round calendar) was marked with rejoicing, dancing, sacrifice, and celebration. The new year was also celebrated, as was the beginning of each month. In Postclassic times, incense, drinks, and loaves of cornmeal and squash seeds were offered to statues of the deities. People also drew blood from their ears and put it on the statues.

Ceremonies were serious affairs, since the fate of the universe rested on pleasing the deities—but with all the feasting and dancing, the Maya must have enjoyed themselves at these festivals too.

Left: *Reclining human figure called a chacmool. The figure holds a stone plate on his stomach as he looks out over the stairs to the Temple of the Warriors in Chichén Itzá. Some people believe the figure may have been an altar where people were sacrificed, or where offerings were made to the gods.*

CHAPTER FOUR

ALL LIFE IS SACRED

The Maya made images of the spirit world in their sculpture, architecture, and paintings. This huge stucco mask from the Pyramid of the Masks in Kohunlich, Mexico, is probably an image of Itzamná, the lord of the heavens and lord of day and night.

Every part of Maya culture—architecture, sculpture, even the calendars and numbers—reflects Maya beliefs. The great Maya cities were not just places to live: The buildings, sculpture, and art were stone-and-paint images of the spirit world. The Maya's everyday life, too, revolved around their beliefs. The ceremonies that filled their lives, the role of the king, even their wars, were all determined by their belief that their purpose in life was to nurture and please the gods.

Living Stories

The myth of the Hero Twins was the heart and soul of Maya culture. In the story extraordinary human beings entered the underworld (Xibalbá), outwitted the gods of death, and returned to life. This story itself was a metaphor for the daily setting of the sun (when it went into Xibalbá) and its triumph over the forces of darkness (when it rose again in the morning).

The Maya acted out this story in dozens of ways, from the pictures they made to the rituals they performed. By doing this, they relived the glories of their mythic ancestors and showed that they, too, could win over the forces of evil.

Sacred Architecture

When we look at Maya cities, we see buildings: tall pyramids, mighty temples, ball courts, and

wide courtyards. To the Maya, though, the buildings were more than buildings—they represented the story of the Hero Twins.

According to Maya belief, the Hero Twins entered the underworld through a cave in a sacred mountain. Think of the shape of a pyramid—it's very much like a mountain. The doorway into the temple on top of the pyramid represented the entrance to the world of the gods—like the entrance to a cave. Symbols and writing on

The nobles of Bonampak wear long white cloaks as they witness the presentation of the heir to the throne, the son of Chan Muan. The painting celebrates the new king, who is the center of communication between the world of human beings and the spirit world.

the temples and pyramids even named them as man-made mountains. Carvings around a temple doorway identified it as the gaping mouth of a reptilelike monster. An example is Temple 22 on the Acropolis at Copán, which dates from the time of 18 Rabbit, the unfortunate king captured by the kingdom of Quiriguá. The temple is carved with glyphs naming it as an artificial mountain, and its outer doorway is framed by a giant mask showing a large, open mouth. When a ruler walked through the temple doorway, he entered the underworld to communicate with the gods.

Every city had its ball court, which represented the scene of the original contest between the Hero Twins and the gods of death.

The ball court at Copán. The ball court was a symbol of the place where the human and supernatural worlds met.

Like the temple doorway the ball court represented an opening into the underworld.

Even the way the buildings were laid out had a spiritual meaning. The royal palaces were at the center of the city, representing the earth in the center of the three-level universe. In the north, which was associated with the heavens and dead rulers, were the shrines and tombs. Between the center and the north was the ball court, the doorway between worlds. This pattern is clear at Cerros, a Preclassic site, and at Tikal, a Classic-period site, where the central palace is separated from funeral shrines in the North Acropolis by a ball court.

Sacred Art

In the Maya world artists did not create paintings and sculptures to express their feelings. Art was created to show the rituals necessary to maintain balance in the universe. Bloodletting, sacrifice, the king communicating with his ancestors and the gods, the ball game—these images occur over and over in carvings on monuments and buildings. The images celebrated these events, and also educated the people as to what was required according to their beliefs.

Art also gave a face to the spirit forces that lived in the visible and invisible worlds. For example, the sun god, or Kinich Ahau ("Lord Sun"), has a face with a straight nose and a square eye. His front teeth are often filed into the shape of a T, and a long hank of hair hangs by his face. This image of the sun god often appears as a breastplate worn by royalty. The most important title given to kings, *mah k'ina* ("great sun lord"), was sometimes written as a picture of this god.

Another purpose of art during the Classic period was to show the bloodline of kings. Proving the king's connection to the founder of the city-state—who was often a mythical ancestor or god—meant he had the right to rule. Many of the images recorded in stone are of parents and ancestors transferring power to their children, usually from father to son.

Over and over, in carvings and paintings, we see images of the birth of an heir, the king taking the throne, and the sacrifice

Maya art reflected Maya beliefs about the universe. Sitting on this vessel from 200–450 C.E., the sun god paddles his canoe across the watery surface of the supernatural world. In Maya belief, canoes carry the dead across the waters from the world of the living to the world of the dead. The sun was believed to descend into the land of the dead at night and to reappear in the morning in the land of human beings.

of captives to seal the event as a sacred moment. Images of the king's death, such as the famous carving on the stone sarcophagus of Pacal at Palenque, show the king going to the underworld after death. It was believed that the king, like the Hero Twins, would triumph over the gods of death—and, like the Hero Twins, rise to the heavens, where he would be worshiped as a god.

Sacred Behavior: The Role of the King

The king is often shown in art—both because it was the king who paid for the art, and because the king was the center of spiritual life for his community. He personally offers blood to the gods; he goes into a trance to have a vision and communicate with the supernatural world; he leads his people in battle when they need a captive to offer to the gods.

The king was the ruler, but he was also the head priest. Through the rituals he performed, the gods were nourished, corn and squash grew, and people could speak with their dead ancestors and the gods. Images of the king were certainly meant to convince the people that he had the right to rule. But they were also spiritual images, since the king was identified with the World Tree, the point of intersection between the natural and supernatural worlds. (On the lid of the sarcophagus of Pacal, for example, Pacal is shown falling along the trunk of the World Tree.)

Maya social life was based on this spiritual image of the king. Just imagine the work that must have gone into building the huge pyramids! Yet the common people were willing to build them, sculptors carved the praises of the king in stone, and artists etched scenes of his life in jade. There is no evidence that the king maintained armies to force the people to do these things (though some researchers believe the king controlled the best farmland, and paid the people with food to do his work). If the people shared the belief that the king was divinely inspired to rule, then he could maintain power without challenge.

A Maya king sits on his throne, an elaborately carved bench. He wears a wide collar and three-paneled cape. His removable headdress is missing, but we can still see the frown and look of concentration on his face.

53

This once brightly painted clay figurine shows a Maya king wearing a feather headdress, royal belt, huge pendants on his chest, decorated apron, and sandals. He carries a round shield on his left wrist. The king was both the ruler and head priest.

In fact, one reason proposed for the collapse of the Maya in the ninth century is that the role of the king changed. He was no longer the representation of the World Tree; he no longer spoke with the gods. A committee of nobles ran the government. Perhaps abandoning their belief in the king as a god and god-communicator led the people to abandon their city centers, which were built around the concept of king as god.

Sacred Numbers and Days

The Maya were excellent timekeepers and astronomers. But they didn't study these things simply for the pleasure of it. They believed that by understanding the cycles of time and space, humans could harmonize their lives with the order of the universe.

For example, the maize-god day (Kan) was good and the death-god day (Cimi) was evil. By knowing which deity governed each day, and keeping track of which day it was, Maya

One of Shield Jaguar's wives helps him dress for battle on February 12, 724 C.E. The king is on the left, wearing cotton armor. His wife hands him a jaguar headdress. Symbols of blood on her face show she has just finished the bloodletting ceremony shown on Lintel 26 from Yaxchilán (see illustration page 44).

IF YOU WERE AN ANCIENT MAYA

If you were born as an ancient Maya, your way of life would be different if you were a noble or a commoner, a boy or a girl. It also would vary depending on where and when you lived. With this chart you can trace the course your life might have taken if you were a commoner living in the Yucatán during Postclassic times (900–1500).

You were born in Yucatán. . . .

As a Boy . . .   **As a Girl . . .**

You probably live in a simple house with stone walls and a thatched roof. Right outside is a small patio for a vegetable garden and fruit trees. You and your parents, young brothers, and sisters all sleep in one room. Until the age of three or four, your mother cares for you.

At age 4 or 5 a small white bead is fastened to your hair, which you wear until about age 13 as a sign of purity. Your father takes over your care and begins training you to be a man.

At age 4 or 5 a string is tied around your waist with a red shell hanging from it, as a sign of purity. You wear this until about age 13.

At about age 13 you participate in a ceremony called the descent of the gods. After a formal ritual, a priest cuts the white bead from your hair as a sign that you can marry.

At about age 13 you participate in a ceremony called the descent of the gods. After a priest performs a ritual, your mother removes the red shell from the string around your waist as a sign that you can now marry.

As a teenager you live in a separate house with other unmarried young men. You paint yourself black, and work with your father in the cornfield.

As a teenager you learn to cook tortillas, weave, and take care of the house. Your mother teaches you to be modest: Whenever you meet a man, you turn your back and step aside to let him pass.

At about age 14 you marry a girl from the same village and social class as you. Your father chooses your wife with the help of a match-maker, and your mother makes clothes for you and your bride.

At about age 14 you marry the man your father has chosen with the help of a match-maker. Your husband comes to live with you in your parents' house for about six or seven years, then you move to a new house near your in-laws' house.

As a husband and father you spend most of your day working in the cornfields. After work you join your family and pray to the ancestors and gods. You wear your hair long and braided, wound around your head with a tail falling behind, and tattoo your hands, face, and body.

As a wife and mother you work at home, cooking, sewing, weaving, raising fowl, and going to market. Sometimes you work along-side your husband in the field. You wear your hair long and tattoo yourself from the waist up.

When you die, your body is wrapped in a shroud and your mouth is filled with ground corn and jade beads for you to use as money in the afterlife. You are buried under the floor of your house, and the house is then abandoned.

56

rulers had the power to avoid trouble. The calendar, then, was a source of spiritual power. The king must have carefully guarded his knowledge of the days and gods, since it gave him power in the eyes of the people.

Numbers too proved that the king had the right to rule. Since the king could count his ancestors back to the beginning of time, he was clearly a representative of the gods—and therefore entitled to rule.

The large numbers of the Long Count were also used to show that a certain day occurred at the same position in the cycle of the moon or Venus as it had done long ago in the days of the Hero Twins. By showing a link between the present and that date in the distant past, the king linked himself to the gods of mythic times.

Sacred History

Maya ceremonies and festivals were seen as a way to actually bring spiritual beings into the physical world. They could also transform a human being into a sacred being.

The king was essential to these ceremonies because he was the World Tree made into a person: He was a bridge between the ordinary world and the sacred world. Since his whole life revolved around nurturing and pleasing the gods, even the historical events in the king's life were considered sacred.

CHAPTER FIVE

THE LIVING MAYA

Modern Maya girls from Chichicastenango, Guatemala, wear colorful woven blouses just as their ancestors did.

The ancient Maya suffered unknown disasters that caused them to abandon their magnificent cities around 900, at the end of the Classic period. At the end of the Postclassic period, in the 1500s, they suffered years of war and diseases inflicted by the Spanish conquerors. And yet, in villages today in southern Mexico, Guatemala, Belize, and Honduras, live people whose faces are so like the faces carved on the stone monuments that they look like cousins. The ancient builders of pyramids did not disappear: Some five million of their descendants still live in the lands of their ancestors. A thousand years after the time of kings and sacred rituals, the modern Maya still preserve many of their ancient customs, ceremonies, and beliefs.

Blending Traditions

Like their ancestors, most Maya today are farmers who live in small, thatched houses around patios with their extended families nearby. They raise corn, weave clothes, and make pottery. Men work in the fields, and women take care of the house and children.

In many ways, of course, the modern Maya lead very different lives from their ancestors. When the Spaniards conquered the Maya's land in the 1500s, they tried to change the Maya into Spaniards. They made Maya children learn Spanish, prohibited the use of the Maya writing system, burned Maya books,

The descendants of the ancient Maya struggle to survive in conditions very different from those of their ancestors. There are no more powerful city-states, no more kings, no more pyramids and temples being raised to the sky. Today many Maya work on plantations where they suffer poverty and malnutrition, and they fear for their lives because of war.

In Guatemala a thirty-year civil war has claimed 100,000 Maya lives, 40,000 people have disappeared, and a million have been exiled from their homes. In 1992 a Guatemalan woman, Rigoberta Menchu, won the Nobel Peace Prize for her struggle for human rights for her people, the Quiché Maya.

Rigoberta Menchu grew up working on coffee and cotton plantations with her family. She saw many people die of malnutrition and pesticide poisoning, including her younger brother. When her father participated in a peaceful demonstration for human rights, he was killed. Then her mother and older brother were tortured and killed by the Guatemalan army. When she spoke up for human rights, her life, too, was threatened. In 1981 she fled to Mexico for safety. Her book *I, Rigoberta Menchu* tells the story of her family and the suffering of the Quiché Maya people. When Rigoberta Menchu won the Nobel Peace Prize, people around the world became aware of the struggles of the modern Maya to survive.

In Mexico the Maya who live in southern Chiapas are demanding that the Mexican government help them improve their lives. There, about fifty-five of every one thousand Maya babies die at birth, eleven times more than the Mexican average. About 69 percent of the Maya are literate, compared to 87 percent in Mexico as a whole. Groups of Maya and non-Maya people have taken up arms to demand jobs, health care, and better education. They are negotiating with the Mexican government for their rights as citizens of Mexico.

Rigoberta Menchu is a Guatemalan Maya who won the Nobel Peace Prize in 1992 for her struggle for human rights for the modern Maya.

Since the early 1980s, many Maya have moved from their native lands to other countries as refugees. Today tens of thousands of Maya live in the United States.

destroyed their religious symbols, and forced them to accept Catholicism. Communication among communities was broken off. Maya culture splintered into many forms, each village preserving its version of the ancient traditions and beliefs.

Modern Yucatec Maya house with a pole-and-thatch roof— just like the Maya houses of a thousand years ago.

Today most Maya are Catholic. But they have not forgotten their ancient beliefs: Instead they have blended them with Christianity. The Christian god is called Our Father Sun and is linked with Kinich Ahau, the Sun-faced Lord of ancient times. The Virgin Mary is called Our Mother Moon or Our Mother Maize. Christ is identified with Hunahpu, the hero of the *Popol Vuh*. The cross itself is worshiped as a god. Besides being a Christian image, it is also seen as an image of the World Tree— a doorway to the houses of the gods.

Modern Maya farmer works in his cornfield in Chiapas, Mexico. Many modern Maya raise crops, cook, and weave garments in the same way their ancestors did.

The modern Maya continue the tradition of shaping pots and vessels from clay as their ancestors did long ago.

The symbols in the homes of the modern Maya show the blending of beliefs that has occurred. On the eastern wall of a Maya home is a cross decorated with pine branches. It celebrates Jesus Christ—and also the rising sun. On the patio, another cross faces west to salute the sun's passage below the earth.

Maya children today attend school in a rural schoolhouse.

Beliefs That Live On

The modern Maya, like their ancestors, believe that the balance between human beings and deities must be maintained to keep order in the universe. They respect nature and offer prayers for the success of their crops. And they believe it is still possible to find doorways to the spirit world. They do this through sacrifice, as did their ancestors—only today they sacrifice chickens, not human beings.

Mountains, mountain passes, rocks, trees, and caves are still considered sacred. The most sacred is a mountain and cave together—just like the artificial holy mountains and caves the ancient Maya created when they built their pyramids and temples. Today many Maya believe that mountains are the homes of ancestor deities they call fathers and mothers, who watch over human beings.

The modern Maya combine elements of their ancient beliefs with Christianity. Here a Maya man tends a shrine with symbols of both traditions.

In Zinacantan, a village in Mexico, the fathers and mothers are seen as distant ancestors of the Maya. They represent the first people who learned how to plant corn, praise their creator, and live as proper human beings. According to myth, the gods at the four corners of the universe ordered them to live inside the mountains. The fathers and mothers watch over their descendants and wait for offerings of black chickens, candles, incense, and liquor. They are very wise and guide the behavior of their people. If someone misbehaves—for example, by fighting with relatives or mistreating corn—the ancestral gods punish him or her.

The people of Zinacantan also believe in the Earth Lord. A fat, greedy god who smokes cigars, he lives underground and has lots of money, herds of cows and horses, and flocks of chickens. He controls rain and lightning, and owns everything on earth.

Stories tell about men who have become fabulously wealthy by going into a cave to visit the Earth Lord. But the Earth Lord can be dangerous: It is said that sometimes he captures a man and forces him to work in the earth for years.

A Guatemalan Maya lights candles in front of an ancient monument in El Baúl, a Pacific coast Maya site that dates back to the Preclassic period.

From Kings to Shamans

The Maya kings are gone, but some of the social roles played in Maya villages today remind us of the ancient customs.

In the highlands most villages have political and ritual

offices called *cargos*. *Cargo* holders and their wives organize religious celebrations and settle community disagreements. It takes a lot of money to be *cargo* holders, since they are responsible for paying for the feasts, flowers, incense, and other things needed for festivals.

These offices are considered a sacred responsibility and an honor. The *cargo* is passed from one man to another in special ceremonies that sometimes include passing a ceremonial staff from one person to another—like a modern version of the staff kings used to hold. It is such a great honor to have a *cargo* that men put their names on a waiting list for one—and are willing to wait twenty years to get it.

In ancient times kings communicated with the gods. Today shamans have that power and responsibility. They perform baptisms and lead masses in churches. They also hold special ceremonies to heal illnesses and predict the future. In several communities shamans still count days according to the 260-day sacred-round calendar. Just like the ancient keepers of the calendar, they consult the calender to determine birthday names for babies and to choose the proper days for ceremonies. Some also still keep the old 365-day calendar with its 18 months of 20 days and its 5 unlucky days.

Ceremonies: Ancient and New

Many communities maintain their connection with tradition by combining ancient ceremonies with Catholicism. When someone is ill, moves into a new home, or is about to take office in the community, villagers make offerings at cross shrines. These ceremonies are called visits to the gods.

Led by a shaman, people gather at a cross shrine at the bottom of a mountain. The shaman lights candles and makes offerings of prayers, incense, food, and liquor. The people then climb to the top of the mountain and offer more prayers and gifts to the gods. These ceremonies are probably like the ones practiced by the ancient Maya when they prayed before stelae and then climbed up the pyramids to pray in the temples on top.

In the ceremony before planting corn, we see how the ancient belief in a four-sided universe has survived—and how it has been combined with Catholic ritual. Cornfields have cross shrines at their four corners and in the center. Each year, before planting corn, a shaman leads farmers in a ritual called candles for the cornfield. The participants walk in a procession to the cross shrines at each corner of the field, and to the center shrine. At each shrine the shaman offers candles and prays to the Earth Lord while incense burns. The men pour liquor on the ground for the Earth Lord and drink some themselves. Then they plant the new crop of corn.

THE BRING-RAIN CEREMONY (CH'A-CHAC)

In Maya villages today, just as in the past, people worry if it doesn't rain. Without rain the crops won't grow and people will go hungry. When this happens the shaman is called to perform a Ch'a-Chac, or bring-rain ceremony. We can see many elements of ancient Maya belief in this ceremony: the four-sided universe, the ancient Chac gods, and the role of incense and prayer.

The men of the village build an altar, a four-sided table of poles tied together with vines. They cover it with a roof of leaves and place a cross made of sticks behind it. Four young men stand at the corners of the altar. They represent the Chacs, the rain gods. They clap wooden sticks together, roar like the sound of thunder, and sprinkle fresh water onto boys who crouch at their feet beside baby corn plants. The boys chirp and croak like frogs after a rainstorm.

The shaman sprinkles incense on burning coals in a tin can and circles around the altar, praying aloud. Sweet incense smoke billows around him, a fragrant smell in the air. His eyes half closed, he raises his voice and calls out to the rain gods. He asks them to send rain and save the farmers' crops. As he finishes, a faint roar of thunder is heard in the distance. It doesn't start to rain right away, but the villagers know that it will soon. Everyone laughs and celebrates by drinking honey wine and feasting on bread and chicken stew.

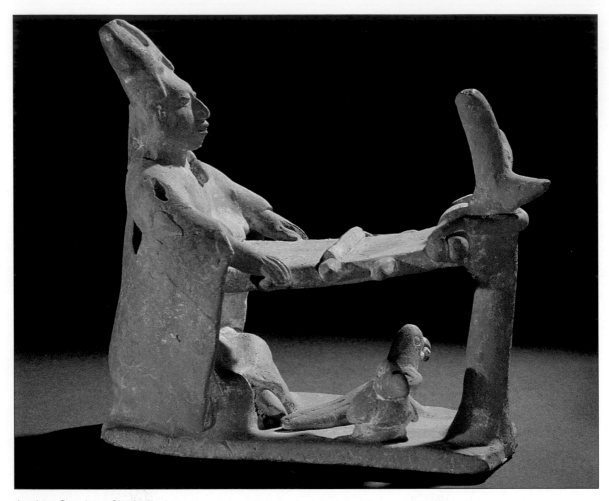

Ancient figurine of a woman weaving with a back-strap loom—the same way Maya women weave today.

Sacred Designs

We have few examples of ancient Maya fabric since cloth is fragile and disintegrates over time. However, from sculptures and the brightly colored wall paintings of Bonampak, we know that weaving was an important art among the ancient Maya. This art is also very much a part of the lives of the modern Maya.

In the highlands of Guatemala, Maya women weave intricate patterns using the back-strap loom. This is a kind of loom in which a cord attached to the loom is passed around the back of the weaver and fastened to a tree or post. A picture in the Postclassic-period Madrid Codex shows the back-strap loom being used by Ix Chebel Yax, the goddess of weaving. This picture lets us know that women of that time—and perhaps earlier—also must have used the back-strap loom.

The patterns woven into the cotton fabric were complicated and rich—just as the fabric woven today has detailed, beautiful patterns. The meaning of the colors used today is believed to be similar to their meaning in ancient times: Yellow represents corn or food, black is for weapons, red is blood, blue is sacrifice, and green is royalty. (Green is the royal color because it is the color of the feathers of the quetzal bird, which were prized by Maya rulers.)

Machine-made fabrics have replaced handwoven ones in many places. But in parts of Guatemala, people can still tell where someone is from just by looking at the pattern of their shirt. This is because each community makes certain traditional designs that have become identified with that village or town.

A modern Maya woman uses a back-strap loom and ancient techniques to make clothes.

The designs, drawn from ancient beliefs, show the connection with old times. Diamond designs refer to the earth and sky. Wavy designs, called snakes or flowers, symbolize the fertile earth with its wealth of plants and animals. Three vertical lines stand for the ancestors or for monkeys. Figures such as toads and saints represent the rain god and the Catholic saints who watch over the world.

The huipil, *a traditional Maya blouse. People can tell where someone comes from by the design on the person's* huipil, *since each community weaves unique designs.*

When a modern Maya woman wears a traditional blouse, or *huipil* (wee-PEEL), that she has woven, she is in the center of a universe that shows her family history, where she lives, the saints that are important to her, and symbols of rain and fertility. Weaving the *huipil* is an art, and it is also a sacred duty ordered by the gods and ancestors. For centuries women have woven gowns for the images of their gods. These gods are today identified with the Virgin and Catholic saints.

Lessons from the Maya

The ancient Maya have left another sort of legacy besides their descendants, arts, and beliefs. Some people say the so-called collapse of the Maya Classic period, when the Maya abandoned their cities and moved north to the Yucatán, has important lessons for us today.

Some researchers believe the Maya population grew so large that the Maya needed more food than they had. The researchers say the Maya cut down the rain forest to provide fields to raise food, without concern for the rain forest itself. These unwise farming methods provided food for a short time, but made the soil useless after a while. Some people say we are in danger of doing the same thing today. They say we can learn from the example of the Maya and be more careful with the resources of the earth.

Another lesson can be found in the Maya sacred book, the *Popol Vuh.* When people were first created, it says, they could see everything. The creator gods thought this gave the people too much power, so the gods clouded their understanding. Like "breath on a mirror," the *Popol Vuh* says—this is how we understand things today. This humble attitude—that we as human beings do not know everything—is a lesson for us all.

We do not know everything about the Maya—and we may never completely understand what their civilization was like. We do not know everything about our own world, either. But perhaps what we learn about the Maya will help us to understand them better—as both an ancient and a living people. And perhaps, if we look closely, we will also learn something about ourselves.

The Ancient Maya: A Time Line

2000 B.C.E.

2000 B.C.E.–250 C.E.
PRECLASSIC PERIOD

c. 2000–1000 B.C.E.
Early Preclassic

c. 2000–1500 B.C.E.
First villages along Pacific coast

c. 1000–400 B.C.E.
Middle Preclassic

c. 1000–750 B.C.E.
Expansion of settlement inland

c. 600 B.C.E.
First architecture and monuments

c. 400 B.C.E.–250 C.E.
Late Preclassic

c. 250 B.C.E.
Writing and Long Count calendar
spread throughout Mesoamerica

Villages grow into city centers

c. 100 B.C.E.–100 C.E.
Cerros built and abandoned,
El Mirador and Tikal built

250–900
CLASSIC PERIOD

c. 250–600
Early Classic

292
First dated
Classic-period monument,
Tikal Stela 29

c. 300–500
First records of kings at Palenque

Early monuments at
Copán and Quiriguá

411
Stormy Sky takes the
throne at Tikal

562
Caracol defeats Tikal

c. 600–800
Late Classic

615–683
Pacal rules Palenque

695
Ah Cacau of Tikal captures
the king of Calakmul,
restoring Tikal's power

CLASSIC
PERIOD

POSTCLASSIC
PERIOD

C.E.   250 C.E.   900 C.E.   1500 C.E.

900–1500
POSTCLASSIC PERIOD

c. 700
Temple of Inscriptions
built at Palenque

738
18 Rabbit of Copán
captured by Cauac Sky
of Quiriguá

763
Yax Pac,
last great king of Copán,
takes the throne

c. 790
Bonampak wall
paintings made

c. 800–1000
Terminal Classic

c. 800–1000
Growth of Puuc-region city-states
such as Uxmal

c. 889
Last dated monument
at Tikal, which was
abandoned soon after

c. 900–1200
Early Postclassic

c. 900
Great lowland
city-states abandoned

c. 1000
Decline of Uxmal

c. 1000–c. 1221
Rise and fall of
Chichén Itzá

c. 1200–1500
Late Postclassic

c. 1221–1450
Rise and fall of Mayapán

1540–1546
Conquest of Maya
by Spaniards

GLOSSARY

bloodletting: cutting oneself on purpose so that blood will flow

celt (sehlt)**:** oval-shaped carving, sometimes of jade. Celts often hung from the belts of nobles.

codex (KOH-deks), an ancient manuscript

codices (KOH-duh-seez)**:** plural of codex

eclipse: partial covering of a star or planet by another heavenly body. An eclipse of the sun happens when the moon passes between the sun and earth, blocking out the sun's light. An eclipse of the moon happens when the earth passes between the moon and the sun, casting its shadow on the moon's surface.

epigraphers: people who decode ancient inscriptions, such as hieroglyphs

hieroglyph: picture or symbol used to represent words or sounds; also called glyph

huipil (wee-PEEL)**:** traditional blouse worn by Guatemalan women

incense: gum, spice, or herb that gives off a pungent smell when it is burned. Maya incense was copal, a sticky gum from trees.

Popol Vuh (POH-pole VOO)**:** sacred book of the Quiché Maya people

sacbe (SAHK-bay)**:** broad roads built by the Maya between cities or ceremonial centers

sarcophagus: stone coffin

shaman: priest believed to be able to contact the spirit world, usually during a trance

stela (STEE-luh), plural **stelae** (STEE-lee)**:** stone tree. Upright carved pillar that stood in rows before temples.

underworld: in Maya belief, the world beneath the earth where gods and the dead lived, and where the sun went at night; called Xibalbá

Xibalbá (shee-bahl-BAH)**:** the Maya underworld

FOR FURTHER READING

Chrisp, Peter. *The Maya.* New York: Thomson Learning, 1994.

Lattimore, Deborah Nourse. *Why There Is No Arguing in Heaven: A Mayan Myth.* New York: Harper & Row, 1989.

Menchu, Rigoberta. *I, Rigoberta Menchu,* ed. Elisabeth Burgos-Debray, trans. Ann Wright. London: Verso, 1987.

Nicholson, Peter. *The Maya: Facts, Stories, Activities.* New York and Philadelphia: Chelsea Juniors, 1994.

Sexton, James D., ed. *Mayan Folktales.* New York: Doubleday, 1992.

Stuart, Gene S., and George E. Stuart. *Lost Kingdoms of the Maya.* Washington, D.C.: National Geographic Society, 1993.

Taube, Karl. *Aztec and Maya Myths: The Legendary Past.* Austin, Texas: University of Texas Press, 1993.

Tedlock, Dennis. Popol Vuh: *The Definitive Edition of the Mayan Book of the Dawn of Life and the Glories of Gods and Kings.* New York: Simon & Schuster, 1985.

Trout, Lawana Hooper. *The Maya,* Indians of North America. New York: Chelsea House, 1991.

BIBLIOGRAPHY

Aveni, Anthony F. *Ancient Astronomers.* Montreal and Washington, D.C.: St. Remy Press and Smithsonian Books, 1993.

Baudez, Claude F. *Lost Cities of the Maya.* New York: Harry N. Abrams, 1992.

Bierhorst, John. *The Mythology of Mexico and Central America.* New York: William Morrow, 1990.

Clendinnen, Inga. *Ambivalent Conquests: Maya and Spaniard in Yucatan, 1517–1570.* New York: Cambridge University Press, 1987.

Culbert, T. Patrick. *Maya Civilization,* Exploring the Ancient World. Washington, D.C.: Smithsonian Books, 1993.

Freidel, David, Linda Schele, and Joy Parker. *Maya Cosmos:*

Three Thousand Years on the Shaman's Path. New York: William Morrow, 1993.

Landa, Friar Diego de, trans. William Gates. *Yucatán: Before and After the Conquest.* Baltimore: The Maya Society, 1937.

Markman, Roberta H., and Peter T. Markman. *The Flayed God: The Mythology of Mesoamerica.* San Francisco: Harper-SanFrancisco, 1992.

Miller, Mary Ellen. *The Art of Mesoamerica from Olmec to Aztec.* New York: Thames and Hudson, 1986.

Miller, Mary, and Karl Taube. *The Gods and Symbols of Ancient Mexico and the Maya: An Illustrated Dictionary of Mesoamerican Religion.* New York: Thames and Hudson, 1993.

Morris, Walter F. *Living Maya.* New York: Harry N. Abrams, 1987.

Schele, Linda. *The Blood of Kings: Dynasty and Ritual in Maya Art.* New York: George Braziller, 1986.

Schele, Linda, and David Freidel. *A Forest of Kings: The Untold Story of the Ancient Maya.* New York: William Morrow, 1990.

Sexton, James D., ed. *Mayan Folktales.* New York: Doubleday, 1992.

Sharer, Robert. *The Ancient Maya,* 5th ed. Stanford, California: Stanford University Press, 1994.

Stephens, John L. *Incidents of Travel in Central America, Chiapas and Yucatán.* 2 vols. 1841. Reprint, New York: Dover Publications, 1969.

Stephens, John L. *Incidents of Travel in Yucatán.* 2 vols. 1843. Reprint, New York: Dover Publications, 1963.

Stuart, Gene S., and George E. Stuart. *Lost Kingdoms of the Maya.* Washington, D.C.: National Geographic Society, 1993.

Taube, Karl. *Aztec and Maya Myths: The Legendary Past.* Austin: University of Texas Press, 1993.

Tedlock, Barbara. *Time and the Highland Maya.* Albuquerque: University of New Mexico Press, 1992.

Tedlock, Dennis. Popol Vuh: *The Definitive Edition of the Mayan Book of the Dawn of Life and the Glories of Gods and Kings.* New York: Simon & Schuster, 1985.

Vogt, Evon Z. *Tortillas for the Gods: A Symbolic Analysis of Zinacanteco Rituals.* Norman, Oklahoma: University of Oklahoma Press, 1993.

INDEX

Page numbers for illustrations are in boldface

ABOUT THE AUTHOR

Irene Flum Galvin is fascinated by the many mysteries of the ancient Maya: their language, which remained undecoded for a thousand years; the poetry of the stories in the *Popol Vuh*; their extraordinary sculpture and architecture; and, most of all, the way the Maya viewed every part of their lives as sacred. In researching this book, she imagined life through the eyes of the ancient Maya, with beliefs, habits, and rules so different from—and yet parallel to—our own. She feels that the story of the ancient Maya is rich in lessons for us today, and hopes to share their fascinating tale with others.

Years ago, Irene Flum Galvin wrote this poem:

> *A child stands staring, fascinated.*
> *She looks through glass (slightly blurry)*
> *at the sandy remains of a child*
> *who once stood staring, fascinated.*

Writing this book made the poem come alive in a new way.

Irene Flum Galvin's books for young readers include *Brazil: Many Voices, Many Faces* (Marshall Cavendish, 1996), *Japan: A Modern Nation with Ancient Roots* (Marshall Cavendish, 1996), *Chile: Land of Poets and Patriots* (New York: Simon & Schuster/Dillon Books, 1990), and *The Rubber Band Boy* (New York State Council for Children, 1977). She also writes magazine articles and novels, and is currently writing a screenplay based on a true story about the Maya. She has a B.A. in Spanish and French from Binghamton University and a masters degree from Harvard University. She is the president of The Communications Connection, a writing and editorial services company in Rochester, New York, where she lives with her husband, Tom, and two children, Rachel and Danny.